POEMS BY RICHARD THOMAS

AVON
PUBLISHERS OF BARD, CAMELOT, DISCUS, EQUINOX AND FLARE BOOKS

IN SILVER TREES and THE LAST POEMS originally appeared in *The Saturday Evening Post*. Copyright © 1973.

AVON BOOKS
A division of
The Hearst Corporation
959 Eighth Avenue
New York, New York 10019

ISBN: 0-380-00539-5

First Avon Printing, November, 1975

AVON TRADEMARK REG. U.S. PAT. OFF. AND IN
OTHER COUNTRIES, REGISTERED TRADEMARK
MARCA REGISTRADA, HECHO EN CHICAGO U.S.A.

Printed in the U.S.A.

PREFACE

Some of these poems date back to 1965. Since it is not my purpose to present a young man's history, I have not placed them in chronological order. They now have gained consciousness, and in the words of Dylan Thomas, they must go out into the world and stand on their own feet.

If they seem to bear no relation to my life as an actor, perhaps that is because the actor exists while he acts, and the poet exists as he writes. If they are personal and concerned primarily with themes of the heart rather than society, I concede to expressions of self-interest.

I owe much to Mr. William Landis and Mr. Donald Hull—two men who made me aware that language is always a living thing. Very special thanks are also due my editor, Robert Wyatt.

RICHARD THOMAS
NEW YORK, 1974

CONTENTS

POSTSCRIPT

When I confessed my poems were love ones mostly,
someone said, What else at twenty could they be?

"Last night ..."
        But I can't write this down.
How, with endless realms spun out above the bed,
my emptiness was tantalized.

The talker, trained in silent conversation by your
    body
and your eyes,
was hushed and sentenced to anticipation.
His tributes died in solitude, and gifts of gladness
    only,
unaccepted in elation,
        made you fond.

Then what's the use of this—
His sketching out perfection with a pencil
              on erasable bond?

Touch me
like a black satin glove;
and I will fade
  and become a single star
  in my own night;
and cold
  and heat
    and wind will fold,
flicker and die
in my dark majesty.
Revolving alone on my throne
        of space,
a terrible king
    of the void.

In silver trees
stars blow past the leaves.
In the night sky I
see a familiar glow.
Along the path is the echo of a laugh
I'm almost afraid to hear again.
And yet . . . ah! Opens up the evening,
                    blooming clouds!

THE BIRTH OF THE HEAT IN NEW YORK CITY

In the bloody afternoon
dust flies heavily on the hot wind.
Faces are red with the death
of the summer sun.
T-shirts mat on sweaty backs,
and the screaming horns of Spanish summer
    weddings
echo
to woo the steaming city night as it falls.

The birth of the heat was masked
by the last cool winds,
which swept me up to tenement roofs
in city joy.
But cool gives way to dust in sweltering air,
and heated winds grow monotonous,
and summer walks grow long
with screaming horns.

Diddle-diddle-dumpling my son, John,
woke up in the morning with his mother gone.
In each early morning haze the streetlights glow,
and lonely are the little boys
waiting in a row.

Shuffling in a broken line, standing by the door,
some are coughing in the cold and some are on the
    floor.
Moving in a circle, moving in a file,
waiting for the candy-seller
coming with a smile.

Smiles are on his charming face, dimples on his
    chin,
laughing as he goes along—giggling within.
Perhaps a belching in the fog, perhaps a strangled
    cry,
the little boys are there again
and each is going to die.

Diddle-diddle-dumpling my son, John,
woke up in the morning with his mother gone.

Never saw the sun shine, only saw the dawn.
Diddle diddle dumpling
my son, John.

WHILE YOU'RE AWAY

as i kiss the air
kissing your
mouth eating your
hair with my burning
eyes
on you in the dark
in you your cat
eyes shine so fine
so fierce with sticky pain
it hurts
come
sprawl up close sweet
slippy baby
wherever you are smile
(sexy) for me in the dark night and
one of these sweet nights baby i

SONG OF HEAVEN WHERE WE FIND IT

Burning bullion of a stammering sigh—
the steam-flung bath the flinch betrays;
and, flushing wildly, wasting washes you;
else rushing through and into darkness
where, as flickered lightening, rolling slays,
crest-and-ebbing in the cob.

A wailing wonder of a twirling double try
then: Toppled spiral spins to blackness, stays;
where pulls toward day to bubble-burst you,
race the neighing larkness
on, so can the winged couplet flaring
last-time blast through love and bear our sob—
                              sobs ever bearing.

WASHINGTON SQUARE PARK EDUCATION

Washington Square Park is a strange place to
come to now
after dark. Is it long lanes of students speaking
low
that makes me squirm inside with knowing you?
Or faces in the summer grass, like reflections in a
dark lake,
reminding me
that you were here too? I still am here, learning
to try.
For what it's worth, I've watched you cry here.

Caught in iron-tooth traps,
animals chew off their feet.
I immolate my heart on my tongue
     even now.
I have talked these midnights
into mortality under hideous bedlamps;
extinguish them now.
Come,
    embrace me with darkness.
Take my words deep inside you
   and unspeak me
       in your eyes.

RICHARD THOMAS

Beauty has gone underground
arm in arm with Pan.
Every essence of each "dead" divinity,
every vestige of polite virginity
has coupled with propriety
and run away from man.
Just this morning jasmine branches rising,
falling, at the bedside window
told me so.
I have been away too long from nature,
mind averted.
I have been too long diverted
by a world of minor stature,
imitation, nomenclature.
and am subject to depreciation
while a social habit keeps me in eclipse.
I have wasted half-long days,
and stayed too long admiring lips
in mastering the petty phrase;
and I am in the habit now,
and do not look into the eyes of nature,
nor hang upon her lips for information.
I am now a prince of minor stature,
imitation, nomenclature.

Just this morning,
jasmine branches tapping at the bedside window
called my ears and then my eyes
and then my body to the windy season:
rain-washed, windswept hillside;
cold and swollen
wildflowers, wet and shaking;
leaf-lips dropping clear liquid;
laughing foliage on bushes bent under the wind.
And thus
the eyes,
tiny eyes and faces,
tiny feet and ears
and even—almost—most translucent legs
and slender silver thighs
and lashes trembling—smiling almost—winking
fierce dark eyes
and little dancing goat-steps barely daring
to emerge in my imagination
sang there:
Come among us for your flirting
while the world is harsh and chilly.
You are not the prince of all deflowering;
there are nymphs as happy with a lily.
But should your desire retain
a gentle reverence for the gentle race,
then shocks of rain against your face will bring
the wild and lonely lenience of spring.

Among us
you may walk
when bark is red
with rain
and earth, pure.
But your tears will flow
as rain,
and a demon's joy
like wind rush through
and above with the sun above.

Among us
find yourself
or what you will be in the rain:
what god or goddess you will play—
the wetness or the faun himself.
But run your course
behind your eyes,
and with a chill
warm yourself and your happiness.

For among us
the muddy taste
of water and fallen leaves

is clean as a spring in fall.
Find your own rain in the wind today.
His is not yours today.

RICHARD THOMAS

FALSE OLYMPIAN

In the stinging salt spray on my exile's raft
I recalled the dying bull without his throne;
and the onward-sailing craft stopped and set
half-mast its colors, not for the strangling bulls,
but sadly for the blooming rose which time
will later wilt and leave alone.

Tortured by a frantic madness
of realms dying beneath a cold and silver moon,
of names calling him vaguely in the darkness
and giant shadows on an empty beach,
my father died one windless August evening.
The darkened heavens wrapped him in his rune.

But I have sailed without my father's banner.
Without his dreams it lay, a useless rag.
And I have thrown his golden scepter
from the rail into the dying sea
of suns that could not blind Olympus.
I shut my eyes against their blinding me.

And I see the bull die, lonely in his memories,
and bless me with succession to his throne.
And I pray: Gods, give this raft an easy journey

from calf to fated rose which time must kill.
Release me from the dreams of Eden,
where my dying king could never rule his fill.

Your art lies
in being always
Aphrodite.
Eyes of the
moon
that turn
the tides
are your eyes—
protectors
of that form
which is directoress
over this blade's observances.

E QUEL REMIR

I (exile out of light)
bring you out of the rain,
the cold rain's touch against these walls
your touch.
Out of the rain
bring your body down
lanced by shadows onto the dark tile.
So.

THE WHITE

Something waited for me,
floating in the shadows of the vanished summer
    corn,
and in the eyes of the black trees.

So I listened;
and the snow breathed softly, moving as a silent
    woman
Changing posture in the light and freezing wind.

She waited in the center of the field, unbroken
beautiful—and
I was first.

From somewhere high above the ground
a winter bird called down—
and I was there.

So I looked up
and saw him, watched him
soaring through the rabbit-gray

and, smiling up into the wind,
I lost myself

and ran into the field,
and spinning circles like a fool,
I tripped up on a hidden root.

The sharp, loud crack against the silence
pulled the whole day down upon me as I fell
and twisted over crashing to the snow and
    grimacing
in sheets of tickling pain.

The shock of ice against my face, the wetness of the
    snow
soaked through and through my clothes and then
    my skin
and all
dissolved.
I struggled in her white embrace,
my broken ankle trapped and blood-soaked
in a vise of cold and heat,
and in a sudden swarm of purple, red and pulsing
    white
and dancing in a sea of pain,
I gasped and squirmed
and she breathed long and hard in freezing pangs
and dancing purple, red and white slithered in a
    harsh caress
which held my body close and stroked it hard and
    swift and madly

in a dream of spiced and boiling waves which
    rolled
and gathered, humped and roaring
                to the tingling distant shore.

The foamy undulating surf grew calm;
the colored madness ebbed and trickled from my
    spine
in humming wisps of aftermath I lay in stillness
and the memory of field grew gray and dark
and flickered into space.

Epochs,
centuries of space without cold or heat
as if nothing and I were one body in the same
    shroud,
one sweetness in the same confection.
And then slowly I could see
and perhaps sat up
and vaguely saw the white
swirling her shawl about the field
and stroking the sky with a frozen laugh,
waltzing naked like a child, singing with the wind.
I think I spoke
or cried
or called, perhaps,
but then lay back to let the wind blow.

Today the field is on fire
   with brilliant gold and rushing green.
The wheat is full
   and waves beneath the throbbing sun.
The grass swims freely,
   and trees sway ponderously in the loving wind.
There is no frozen soul amid such summer beauty.
   But copperheads are smiling
in the corn.

RICHARD THOMAS

TWO LYRICS

When I first took you for a walk,
frozen blossoms lay beneath the white.
Snowdrifts hid each thistle stalk,
and bitter winds blew in a winter's night.

And now, on summer walks with you,
the summer fades and dies.
The warm dusk wind is blowing through:
I see a snowfall in your eyes.

Dead leaves fall where cherries fell;
    fallen, find a quiet death
where cherries bud.
Dying, leaves pass loving,
    leaving life that springs the tree
toward heaven.
I fall away from pleasure, as a leaf,
    and hit the ground.

The change of season etched in stone,
of dropped leaf to compost in song,
of climates, dictate living tempi.
What a fool, without an eye for beauty,
I have been without your warm directions:
reading this or reconstructing that in petty phrase,
regardless of the form; form conscious minus heart;
blind in spring, a boring squanderer of precious
    days;
a wanderer through roses with no will.
And now, an empty, thought-blown tool with some
    poetic duty,
I hear music somewhere in this place.
Are you the source?
Gone from me, part of me, your face is the same.
And, dormant, I am the same.

Shadows kiss;
scent remembers.
Give me back my face in your eyes.
What would live without you dies.
Remember this:
In burnt Septembers,
hollow Mays, the precious days evolve,

and keep and sweeten in our history.
Forgotten only breeds remembered mystery
with no resolve.

WOODCUT PLEA

Hold out the shining,
quivering touch,
the shower-bursts, resplendent
in this place.
Set free the blue-steel glows.
Bleed them onto the crushing of points
    and echo them in the psalmody of eyes
      already fading
      in the grain.

RICHARD THOMAS

THE LAST POEM

Ice is the memory of passion frozen on an eastern
     wind;
its fragrance obliterated moments from a lost kiss,
its love-shadows vanished into a freezing dawn
demanding silence.
I recall your touch, restrained beyond compassion,
and it is better lost than barely felt.

SLEEP

I

Arose and remembered a dream:
Where now?
Finest nude
whose nipples and soft belly shame satin,
how were you distinguished?
Richest flesh, refusing rude
silk, ripple gently. Come as matins
with the night extinguished.
I have seen you in the moonlight;
we have drowned before in dreams.
And what passes under candlelight
is so seldom what it seems.
Enfold, flutter and melt me
as you wish, for your desire is always kind.
Gentle, riding bodies may have dealt me love,
but only your sweet contours chart my mind.
With you, eternity is wrought into each hour,
and in the morning you are sweet
when they are sour.

This dream arose remembered,
lost in all but phantom passion

unfolding on the fading sheet,
perspiring in the morning heat.
The sun shines.

II

She is so seldom what she seems
to be before the light is out.
The doubt was there,
the error, old and obvious,
but the old fear followed. The unconquered
remained a fly in the ointment.
The unused art, the uncreased bed,
the night remained.
And the house remained—
a silent theater of possibility and dreams.

Teasing rhythms
move where air is thick with night;
and play where tears have spilt.
From the silvered black outside the frame,
around the softly heaving shoulders,
tangled raven hair,
they romp on little notes of salty hate.
The slowly trickling brine
shines on smallish ivory breasts,
damp and ghostly in the moonbeams—
the tight embarrassed beauty of a child

angry in a silence,
a newly naked viper with no game,
no dream.

RICHARD THOMAS

THE LOVER BEFORE DAWN

(minnow slivers, moon-made
and soft slight-almonds,
rimslides glowing in the slat-light)
Slipping down the soft edge
into the hill-glow
he strokes, in a slow mood,
the soap-milk landscape.
Outrunning the dawn
he searches for signs of life.
Expectant.

I will get up in the morning
not yawning.
I will get out of bed
in the cold in my bear feet
and go to the basin.
I will break the ice with my fist
and wash my face and hands in the bitter water.
But you will stop me with my name;
and I will come crush you in the fur
till winter's end.

THE ONLY WAY

Silver streak
         on holy white
the sun ascending
         in the eye.
Airplane fly
         and bird below
a speckling over lake and tree.
         Across the wing
             the sea of sky
                from God's eye-
              view.

To fall
    still rising high
is heaven
  mine at last.

Curling foam rolls to leeward
through dreams of the gray day.
Her silver band drops to the shore-sand
under that sky. Dropped
to the knees on that cold sand,
my searching yields the sea.
Her silver band melts into the shore-sand
and all is free.
Memory resides.

All gifts go forth.

She cries
and stretches forth her finger which has lost the
    little ring.
She folds, unfolds her hand,
cries and curls back
her finger which has lost the little ring.

All gifts go forth to oblivion.

Cool steps, dyed berry-red,
usher to this small house.
Cats abound. Music on the air
greets company. Coffee always fresh is there,
and cigarettes for the smoker. Long-stemmed
freshcut flowers might be on the table and half-read
the newspaper of a weekend. Proof
of a cultured
spirit.

Inside,
I taste the salt air of islands all around.
Did we bear back gods in this close room?
Will love be part of the bargain
when I am at this desk, writing?

I taste the salt air of islands all around.
The wind's heart blown out by her beauty;
her fragrant body torments wave and rock.
The dull sun, damaged, pays her brave skin hom-
    age
and the salt tastes of her thighs.
I feel these clouds roll in;
this beach a battlefield.

Sudden desire, reaching beyond the reef into chill
        depths
explodes this seascape
and this inhabitant.

Love has no part in the bargain
and she is opaque in her vividness,
a cool figment,
naked
and rejecting.
In front, there is a wall,
a lamp,
        a boat of horn
and boredom.

CHRISTINA

Eyes—
    the first I've looked into
    since long before—
so black
    and deep with fire beyond
the fair face.

Hair
    matching in darkness—veils
    the far shore,
masks
    the depth and drowns the asker
seeking grace.

Your lips
    portend a smile and kiss
    within a pout.
The word,
    drawn deep on Cupid's bow
and barely shot,

lifts
    my face in silence
    to search out

omens
    born of Beauty's doubt,
and long forgot

in haste.

RICHARD THOMAS

How does he play?
Alone.
Blue-lit and smoky, blow
to a rolling continuo.
Across the club, a blonde
with smoke and amber drink
reclines in shadow and purple spill—
a demonstration of the heart's desire
in alcohol and ice.
The cornet swims a stroke of tension
long in the pit of the stomach,
convoluted in the groin,
and purple.
She leans. Her move is cool,
through the light and back again,
and the kid is blue again.

HOOKING UP

I know her apartment:
the hanging lamps, the fur rugs
and the telephones; she has two—
modern in the bedroom
old-fashioned in the kitchen.
When I call her she picks up in the kitchen.
I know she is there because her radio is on.
Her voice gives me great peaceful thrills
as I stand on the tiles of my room
in the sunlight and the breeze and listen.
It is like water on a hot day.
She wants to change phones,
so she leaves the receiver on the small kitchen table
without hanging up
and walks out to the bedroom, singing.
I hear her voice going, trailing off
light and soft like the sunlight on my face.
I listen to it vanish through the house,
spill like breeze in the sun, fly from me
and flow to me in the bedroom where I
wait on the other extension.
And I am in two places, now, listening
from two rooms, and between my ears
is her bed on which she lies. I listen

to the springs on which she bounces, holding me
near where the phone is by her bed at the other
    end of the line
from me where I hover with her floating in the
    morning
in apartments as the close-and-distant muffled
    voices
splash in sunlit air and roll together in the bedroom
and the kitchen where she is because I listen to her
there though I can't hear her there from here
and flying talk below the selves from where the
    mumbling plummets
and she says:

> "Darling, I just got out of the bath,
> and I'm dripping wet all over the bed."

Face against the cold
wet streetlamp
listening.
My kiss of thought
lies blasted on the threshold.
Kissing life
lies tickling in my feet;
and through the window
tempting colors
flashing teeth and smiles
and kisses under fallen hair
and fallen eyes
and face
against the cold wet
lamp post listening.
Someone says, Perhaps
tomorrow when the time is right,
of course.
About-face
before a tear can freeze
against the wind.
Then down the street
with kiss of snow on shuffling feet.

RICHARD THOMAS

Beneath the cold dawn
in the wet pasture
warm cows chew and low.
While at the gate chopped alder
bleeds on dying clover;
even the chill as the sun rolls over
dies and goes.
Bitter, the song of earth
captured in times and spaces.
Sad the tune of fields
forever beside the sun.
Dying sun, cooling in freezing paces,
withering to gathered ashes—
ashes, blown to far-strung places,
your song is difficult.
So difficult.

Power nor of words nor music,
lover.
You are the written hero,
unwritten.

IL MIGLIOR FABBRO

Chart the flight of ecstasy toward the dawn.
Mark the warmth of passion by the afterward.
In languor, civilize desire. In heat, guard
genius. In memory or else anticipation,
dream the faun.

Politic description tends the crypt,
each stone cut in contemplation,
every point of architecture neatly stripped
of any hint at sweet exaggeration.
Only pathos haunts the columns and the lines.
Just this ghost of passion passion's paradise defines.

BELLEDI

Every evening drinking, smiling
winds his way into her heart
and out again by morning.
In the dark place knowing, warning
heart of hearts that in his verse
he fans cold flame,
he finds she ends up slightly worse
for beauty by the light of day. But all the same,
Maria
is a shining wave.
A veil separates the world
from heaven. Dollar bills, deftly curled
into the cleft of her breasts are treasure.
Ringing coins, encompassing those olive moons
and gleaming on the dark sea of her hips
are without price. Her lips
are pleasure! As music lost among cold pines
his heart is lost in the deep mines of love.
Lonely on the mountainside thereof
he marks the far thunder.
Lonely in the night thereof he wonders,
does she love, or is he lost?
Through curtains and the bad light of bars

she dances mystery into his night.
She must be mistress to the thousand stars,
his princess of delight.

JOB

not because of said or did
sent or saved to send
upward downward
out
  out
    alone and
            out
not because of gold or fire
in me or my or this or that
that this could be my gift
from
  bearing
      boring
            awe
confuse
      misuse and
            lose
stammer yes no
or mine or his
these do not do
there
    only is

FALL

Autumn's moonlight
brings our phantoms to the town.
Your face glows through the passing clouds,
and a dream of us long before
is monumental in the breathless sky.
Hope is shattered,
heaven shuttered from the dome.
Stars watch with stale eyes
the passing of our hollowness.
The wandering of twin ghosts through the streets
separated by angles of emptiness from the sky
from each other.
Nights like these, their home
forever.

At day's end
the seeds of the scrub
are blown far
by the night's cool air,

               and
               the ready seeds
               drift on
               to the peak of the furnace,
            where

its blinding figment—
subtle, liquid, distant—
burns to an approaching sun,

               a blazing mass
               the falling morning star
            which

circles this,
its universal speck,
but once, then is gone.

               And this must
               be home.

STOOD-UP

Fool,
every hour by his watch an ache,
makes minutes sad songs.

Fool, sing:
Separated from the question,
banished from the answer coming,
on either side hours of dream

       . . . console me.

"Wedded to his day of waiting,
without pen or sheet, creating verse
he sings; and wiser poets hear."
Foolish by association.

It may not properly amount to much,
this low-brow drama of the windy season.
Perhaps the poet only here defends
himself against himself, or makes amends
for constant conquest and experience.
Or maybe here he just pursues his art
in slight retaliations of the heart.

NOTES

Note to *"Belledi"*:

> I am a great admirer of Arabic music and the art of *Belledi* (or belly-dancing as it is frequently called), and have been since a friend and I stumbled unaware into a small and wonderful club at the eastern end of Hollywood. Indeed, when I travel from town to town, I know the best place to find immediate hospitality is that establishment where the veiled lady dances and the intricate art of the *oud* and *durbekkeh* are practiced.

Note to "Song of Heaven Where We Find it":

> This song is dedicated to Gerard Manley Hopkins, although the subject is perhaps one on which he does not touch in his verse.

Note to "Woodcut Plea":

> Collecting artworks is a passion with me, and this song is dedicated to the woodcut which, when well executed, I consider to be the most desirable of the graphic forms.

Note to *"E Quel Remir"*:
>   This song is dedicated to the Provençal trou-
>   badours, and to Ezra Pound who brought them
>   to life for me.

Note to "Beneath The Cold Dawn":
>   Alder is sacred to the god Bran, and is sym-
>   bolic in this poem of his ritual castration by a
>   rival under the supervision of the Mother
>   Goddess. Needless to say, the poem is dedi-
>   cated to Robert Graves.

INDEX OF FIRST LINES

THE BIG BESTSELLERS
ARE AVON BOOKS!